I0088251

Crocheted Christmas Ornament Covers 3

Susan M Allen

© 2010 by Susan M. Allen. All rights reserved. No part of this book may be reproduced or transmitted in any form or by any means, electronic or mechanical, including photocopying, recording, or by any additional storage or retrieval system, without written permission of Susan M. Allen.

I have made every effort to ensure that these instructions are accurate and complete. I cannot, however, be responsible for human error, typographical mistakes, or variations in work.

Other books by Susan M Allen:

Crocheted Christmas Ornament Covers
Crocheted Christmas Ornament Covers 2

Published by:
Susan M. Allen, 670 Eden Brook Lane, Cordova, TN 38018
901-831-6062
www.SueAllenCrochet.com

Abbreviations

ch........ Chain
beg.......beginning
dc.........double crochet
hdc.......half double crochet
sc.........single crochet
sl st .....slip stitch
sp.........space
tc..........triple crochet
yo.........yarn over

Hook Size

All patterns were completed with steel
hook size 5 (1.7 mm)

Thread

The photographed items were made using
Twilleys Goldfingering thread imported from
England. This can be found on my web site.
The sparkle is unbelievable and does not unravel.
It has a bit of stretch and makes it easy to pull up
around ornament snuggly.

This thread is comparable in size to
#10 thread.

Ornaments

The ornaments used for these patterns
are 2 5/8 inch diameter.

Ornament # 1

Ornament #1

Ch 6, join with sl st to form a circle.

Row 1: Ch 3, 13 dc in circle, join with sl st in top of beg ch-3.

Row 2: Ch 3, dc in same sp, ch 2; * 2 dc in next dc, ch 2, repeat from * around ending with ch-2; sl st in ch-3 of beg ch-3.

Row 3: Sl st to beg of ch 2; ch 3, 2 dc in same sp, ch 2, * 3 dc in next ch 2 sp, ch 2, repeat from * around, ending with ch 2; sl st in ch 3 of beg ch-3. (14 ch-3)

Row 4: Ch 3, keeping last loop on hook, dc in next 2 dc, yo and pull through loops, [cluster made]; ch 7, * sk next ch 2 sp & 3 dc; in next 3 dc make cluster, ch 7, repeat from * around ending with ch-7; sl st in base of first ch-7. (7 clusters)

Row 5: Ch 1, (4 sc, ch 3, 4 sc) in ch 7 sp and in each ch 7 space around; sl st in beg ch-1.

Row 6: Ch 1, sc in next 4 sc, *(sc, ch 15, sc) in same ch-3 sp, 8 sc to next ch-3 sp, repeat from * around ending with 4 sc, join with sl st in beg ch 1.

Finish: Sl st in next 4 sc and to middle of ch 15, sc in top of same ch 15, tie off leaving a long enough tail to gather chained loops, pulling them around neck of ornament. #

#Tie off for this and all the ornament covers in this book; I leave about a 6 inch tail and pull it up through the last sl st. I pull that thread through all the loops and pull it snug around the neck of the ornament. I do this around the ornament 3 or more times then I weave down through one of the ch loops to about the middle of the ornament and then cut. The reason I go around the ornament neck 3 or more times is that if the ornament breaks I have plenty left to put on a new ornament.

Ornament # 2

Ornament #2

Ch 6, join with sl st to form a ring.

Row 1: Ch 6, (dc in ring, ch 3) 5 times; join with sl st in 3rd ch of beg ch-6.

Row 2: Ch 1, (sc, hdc, 3 dc, hdc, sc) [group] in each ch 3 sp around ending with sc; sl st in ch 1 of beg ch 1.

Row 3: Ch 3, dc in same sp, ch 6, do 2 dc between each group around then ch 6; join with sl st to 3rd ch of beg ch 3.

Row 4: Sl st to beg of ch-6; (ch 3, 2 dc, ch 3, 3 dc) in ch-6 sp, (3 dc, ch 3, 3 dc) in each ch-6 sp around; sl st in ch-3 of beg ch-3.

Row 5: Sl st to ch-3 sp, ch 10, sc in next ch 3 sp , ch 10, repeat around; sl st in base of beg ch 10.

Row 6: Ch 3, 5 dc, ch 3, 6 dc. In each ch 10 space around (6 dc, ch 3, 6 dc) ending with dc; join with sl st at top of first ch 3.

Row 7: Sl st to middle of ch 3, ch 10, sc in top of next ch 10, ch 10; repeat around ending with ch 10, sl st in base of beg ch 10.

Finish: Sl st to middle of ch 10. sc in top of same ch 10, tie off leaving a long enough tail to gather chained loops, pulling them around neck of ornament. #

See ornament 1

Ornament # 3

Ornament #3

Ch 6, Join with sl st to form a ring.

Row 1: Ch 3, (counts as first dc) 17 dc in ring; join with sl st in top of beg ch 3. (18 dc)

Row 2: Ch 4, (dc in next dc, ch 1), around ending with ch-1; sl st in ch 3 of beg ch 4.

Row 3: In next ch 1 sp, (ch 3, 2 dc, ch 3, 3 dc) *sk 2 ch 1 spaces; in next dc, (3 dc, ch 3, 3 dc) repeat from * around ending with sl st in ch 3 of beg ch 3.

Row 4: Sl st to 1st ch 3 sp, work *(sc, ch 13, sc, ch 11, sc, ch 13, sc) in ch 3 sp, ch 3, sc in space between next 6 dc, ch 3, repeat from * around ending with ch 3, sl st in base of 1st ch 13.

Row 5: Sl st in first 5 ch of next 13 ch, ch 1, 3 sc in same ch 13 sp, (3 dc, ch 2, 3dc) in ch 11 sp, 3 sc in next ch 13 sp; work 3 sc in next ch 13 sp, (3 dc, ch 2, 3dc) in ch 11 sp, 3 sc in next ch 13 sp around ending with 3 sc in last ch 13 sp, join with sl st in beg sc.

Row 6: Sl st across to first ch-2 sp, ch 3, (1 dc, ch 2, 2 dc) * in ch 2 sp; ch 3, sc in sp between group of sc, ch 3,(2 dc, ch 2, 2 dc) in ch 2 sp around, join with sl st in ch 3 of beg ch-3.

Row 7: Sl st to first ch-2 sp, * (2 sc, ch 10, 2 sc) in next ch 2 sp, ch 3, sc in next sc, ch 3,* repeat from * around ending with ch 3, join at beg sc.

Finish: Sl st to middle of ch 10. sc in top of same ch 10, tie off leaving a long enough tail to gather chained loops, pulling them around neck of ornament. #

See ornament 1

Ornament # 4

Ch 6, Join with sl st to form a ring.

Row 1: Ch 1, 11 sc in ring, join with sl st in first ch 1. (12 sc)

Row 2: Ch 3, dc in each sc around; sl st in ch 3 of beg ch 3. (12 dc)

Row 3: Ch 4, dc in same sp; in each dc work (dc, ch 1, dc) [v stitch made], sl st in ch 3 of beg ch 4. (12 v stitch)

Row 4: Sl st to middle of first ch 1 space, ch 4, dc in same space, work (dc, ch 1, dc) in each ch 1 space around; sl st in ch 3 of beg ch 4.

Row 5: Sl st to next ch-1 sp; ch 3, keeping last loop of each dc on hook, 2 dc in same ch-1 sp, yo and pull through loops, [cluster made], (ch 3, cluster, ch 3) in each v stitch around ending with ch 3, sl st in top of first cluster. (12 clusters)

Row 6: Ch 1, 2 sc in ch-3 sp; 3 sc in each ch 3 sp around ending with sc, join with sl st to first ch 1.

Row 7: * Ch 2, sk 2, 3 dc in next sp, ch 2, sk 2, sc in next sp, repeat from * around ending with ch-2, join with sl st to base of first ch-2.

Row 8: Ch 4, dc in same sp, *ch 1, 3 dc in <u>each</u> of next 3 dc, ch 1, dc, ch1, dc, in next sc, repeat from * around ending with ch 1; join with sl st in ch 3 of beg ch 4.

Row 9: Ch 3, sc in ch 1 space of v stitch, * sc in next 5 dc, ch 12, sc in same space, sc in next 4 dc, sc in v stitch, ch 3, sc in same space, repeat from * around ending with sc, join with sl st to beg sc.

Finish: Sl st to middle of ch 12, sc in top of same ch 12, tie off leaving a long enough tail to gather chained loops, pulling them around neck of ornament. #

see ornament 1

Ornament # 5

Ornament #5

Ch 6, Join with sl st to form a ring.

Row 1: Ch 1, 9 sc in ring, join with sl st in first ch 1. (10 sc)

Row 2: Ch 3, * sc in next sc, ch 3, repeat from * around; join with sl st in base of first ch 3. (10 ch 3 spaces)

Row 3: Sl st to middle of ch 3, * ch 4, sc in next ch 3; repeat from * around ending with ch 2, dc in base of first ch 4 to create last ch 4.

Row 4: Ch 4, *sc in next ch 4, ch 4; repeat from * around ending with ch 2, dc in base of first ch 4 to create last ch 4.

Row 5: Ch 5, * sc in next ch 4, ch 5; repeat from * around ending with ch 5, join with sl st in base of first ch 5.

Row 6: Ch 5, * sc in next ch 5, ch 5; repeat from * around ending with ch 3, tc in base of first ch 5 to create last ch 5, join with sl st in base of first ch 5.

Row 7: Ch 1, * in next ch 5 space (4 sc, picot, 3 sc), repeat from * around ending with sc, join with sl st in first sc.

Row 8: Ch 20 , sk 3 sc, picot and 2 sc, *sc in next sc, ch 20, repeat from * around ending with ch 20, sl st in base of first sc.

Finish: Sl st to middle of ch 20, sc in top of same ch 20, tie off leaving a long enough tail to gather chained loops, pulling them around neck of ornament. #

See Ornament 1

Picot– Ch 3, sl st into first ch

Ornament # 6

Ornament #6

Ch 5, Join with sl st to form a ring.

Row 1: Ch 3, 11 dc in ring, join with sl st in ch 3 of first ch 3.

Row 2: Ch 1, sc in same ch as joining, *ch 4, sk next dc, sc in next dc, repeat from * around ending with ch 4, join with sl st in base of beg ch 4. (6 ch 4 loops)

Row 3: Sl st in next 2 chs of next ch 4 loop, ch 5, dc in same sp, ch 3, work (dc, ch 2, dc, ch 3) in each loop around ending with ch 3, join with sl st in ch 3 of first ch 5.

Row 4: Sl st to middle of ch 2, ch 5, dc in same sp, ch 4, work (dc, ch 2, dc, ch 4) in each loop around ending with ch 4, join with sl st in ch 3 of first ch 5.

Row 5: Repeat row 4.

Row 6: Sl st **in** next ch 2 sp, ch 3; in same sp work (2 dc, ch 2, 3 dc); ch 2, sc in next ch 4 loop, ch 3, sl st in sc just made; [picot made] sc, ch 2, * in next ch 2 sp work (3 dc, ch 2, 3 dc) ch 2, sc in next ch 4 loop, ch 3, sl st in sc just made, sc, ch 2, repeat from *around ending with ch 2, join with sl st in ch 3 of first ch 3.

Row 7: Sl st to middle of ch 2, *ch 15, sc in next ch 2, repeat from * around ending with ch 15, sl st in base of first ch 15.

Finish: Sl st to middle of ch 15, sc in top of same ch 15, tie off leaving a long enough tail to gather chained loops, pulling them around neck of ornament. #

See Ornament 1

Ornament # 7

Ornament #7

Ch 6, Join with sl st to form a ring.

Row 1: Ch 3, 9 dc in ring, join with sl st in ch 3 of beg ch 3.
(10 dc)

Row 2: Ch 3, dc in same sp, ch 2; (2 dc , ch 2) in each dc around
ending with ch 2, sl st in ch 3 of beg ch 3.

Row 3: Sl st to first ch 2, ch 3, 2 dc in same sp, ch 2, work
(3 dc, ch 2) in each ch 2 sp around ending with ch 2, sl st in
ch 3 of first ch 3.

Row 4: Ch 3, keeping the last loop on the hook, dc in next 2 dc,
yo and pull through loops, [cluster made], ch 4, work cluster,
ch 4 in each 3 dc around ending with ch 4, sl st in top of first
cluster. (10 clusters)

Row 5: Ch 3, 2 dc in ch 4 sp, ch 2, 3 dc in same ch 4 sp, work
(3 dc, ch 2, 3 dc) in ch 4 spaces around ending with dc, sl st in
top of beg ch 3.

Row 6: Sl st to first ch 2 sp, *ch 15, sc in same ch 2 space ,
sc across next 6 dc, sc in ch 2 sp, repeat from * around ending
with sc, sl st in base of first ch 15.

Finish: Sl st to middle of ch 15, sc in top of same ch 15, tie off
leaving a long enough tail to gather chained loops, pulling them
around neck of ornament. #

See Ornament 1

Ornament # 8

Ornament #8

Ch 8, Join with sl st to form a ring.

Row 1: Ch 3, 2 dc in ring; work ch 3, 3 dc, 5 times in ring, ending with ch 3; join with sl st in ch 3 of first ch 3. (6 groups of ch 3)

Row 2: Sl st to first ch 3 sp, ch 3, 4 dc in same sp, work 5 dc in each ch 3 sp around ; join with sl st in ch 3 of beg ch 3. (30 dc)

Row 3: Ch 1, *sc in next 4 dc, ch 8; repeat from * around ending with ch 8, join with sl st to first ch 1.

Row 4: Ch 1, in next ch 8 work 3 dc cluster; *keeping the last loop on the hook; yo, insert hook in sp, yo and pull up a loop, yo and draw through 2 loops on hook, repeat from * 2 *more* times, yo and pull through all 4 loops on hook, [cluster made], ch 2, work 4 more (3 dc clusters, ch 2) in same ch 8 loop, ch 2; work 5 (3 dc cluster, ch 2) in each ch 8 loop around. This will have a ch 2 connecting each group of 5 cluster groups. End with ch 2, sl st to first ch 1.

Row 5: *Sc in 1st ch 2 sp, ch 3, sc in same sp, sc in next ch 2 sp, ch 3; in top of next (third cluster of group) cluster (sc, ch 18, sc) in each of next 2 ch 2 sps, (sc, ch 3, sc) ch 2, sc in first ch 2 of next cluster; repeat from * around ending with ending with ch 2, sl st in top of first sc.

Finish: Sl st to middle of ch 18, sc in top of same ch 18, tie off leaving a long enough tail to gather chained loops, pulling them around neck of ornament. #

See Ornament 1

Ornament # 9

Ch 4, Join with sl st to form a ring.

Row 1: Ch 3, 9 dc in ring, join in ch 3. (10 dc)

Row 2: Ch 1, sc in same ch as joining, ch 11, sk next dc, * sc in next dc, ch 11, sk next dc, repeat from * around ending with ch 11, join in base of 1st ch 11. (5 ch 11 loops)

Row 3: Sl st in next 5 chs of ch 11 loop, ch 3, dc in same ch, ch 3, sk next ch, 2 dc in next ch, ch 3; * 2 dc in 5th ch of ch 11 loop, ch 3, sk next ch, 2 dc in next ch, ch 3; repeat from * around ending with ch 3, join in 3rd ch of beg ch 5.

Row 4: Sl st in next dc and in next ch 3 loop, ch 1, sc in same loop, ch 3, sl st in sc just made [picot made], sc, ch 9; *sk next ch 3 , sc in next ch 3 loop, ch 3, sl st in sc just made, sc, ch 9; repeat from * around ending with ch 9, sl st in sc of first sc.

Row 5: Sl st to 2 ch of ch 9 loop, ch 3, dc in same ch; (ch 2, sk next 2 chs, 2 dc in next ch) twice; ch 3, sk next picot, 2 dc in 2nd ch of ch 9 loop, (ch 2, sk next 2 chs, 2 dc in next ch) twice; ch 3, sk next picot; repeat from * around ending with ch 3, join in 3rd ch of beg ch 3.

Row 6: Sl st in next dc, in next 2 chs and in next dc; ch 3, dc in same dc as last sl st made; ch 3, 2 dc in next dc; ch 4, skip next ch 3 and 2 dc, sc in next ch 3 loop, ch 3, sl st in sc just made [picot made], sc in same ch 3 loop, ch 4, sk next 2 dc, * 2 dc in next dc, ch 3, 2 dc in next dc, ch 4, skip next ch 3 and 2 dc, sc in next ch 3 loop, sl st in sc just made [picot made], sc in same ch 3 loop, ch 4, sk next 2 dc; repeat from * around ending with ch 4; join in ch 3 of beg ch 3.

Row 7: Sl st to first ch 3, ch 10; *sc in next ch 3, ch 10; repeat from * around ending with ch 10, sl st in base of first ch 10.

Finish: Sl st to middle of ch 10, sc in top of same ch 10, tie off leaving a long enough tail to gather chained loops, pulling them around neck of ornament. #

See Ornament 1

Garland Pattern

Size 10 thread.

9 ft beaded garland needs 150 yards.

18 ft beaded garland needs 300 yards.

Above is approximate yardage, depending on your gauge.

Purchased beaded garland-thread is worked between beads.

Check for sizes, comes in 4 mm up to 8 mm. This pattern is

worked with 6mm. (I buy these beaded garlands at a craft or

Christmas Store. I have also seen them on spools in sewing

stores.)

Size 5 (1.70 mm) steel crochet hook.

Row 1: Sl st in space between 1st and 2nd beads, ch 4, this may vary depending on the type of thread and size of bead-8 mm beads, ch 5, needs to fit snug across bead) sc in between next 2 beads across to end. Turn.

Row 2: Working in chains just completed: (ch 1, sc in first ch-4 sp) * in next ch-4 sp (dc, ch 1, dc, ch 1, dc, ch 3, dc, ch 1, dc, ch 1, dc) shell made, sc in the next ch-4 sp, repeat from * across. Ch 3 turn.

Row 3: Sc, ch 3 in each ch-1 sp and ch-3 sp of the shell, this creates the ruffle effect, sc between shells. Ch 4 turn.

Row 4: On the other side of the bead: sc between beads, ch 4 across. Tie off.

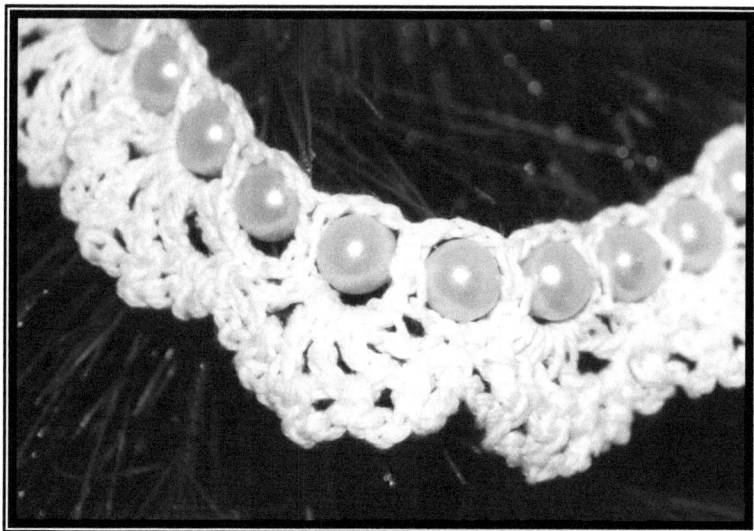

www.ingramcontent.com/pod-product-compliance
Lightning Source LLC
Chambersburg PA
CBHW040347060426
42445CB00029B/35